YOUI

Your Dog & Your Baby
- A Practical Guide -

by Silvia Harmann-Kent

Illustrations by Zak

**First Edition - First Printing
1990**

A Doghouse Publication

YOUR DOG & YOUR BABY
A Practical Guide

First published in 1990
by Doghouse Publications

Phototypeset in Trinity Special

Produced in Great Britain by
Edgebury Press, Eastbourne,
East Sussex

CONTENTS

ACKNOWLEDGEMENTS

I would like to take this opportunity to thank all those who helped me and without whom this book would not have been completed.

My grateful thanks to:

Brian, my husband, and Alexander, my son, for their patience and support when I was still working on the manuscript;

Baby Stephen for providing me with excellent first hand experience regarding dogs and babies;

My beloved parents, Jutta and Karl-Heinz Hartmann, for always being right behind me, no matter what;

My dear parents in law, Thelma and Leslie Kent, for all their day to day practical assistance;

My friend and partner, Rowna Wyatt, for her never failing help and encouragement;

John Fisher for his expert advice and guidance;

All my friends at BOA for always being there when I needed them.

Lastly, to my dear companions past and present:

Seetah, Rio, Sunny, Tina, Sally, Rani and Sweep.

Foreword

In this priceless guide, Silvia Hartmann-Kent combines her knowledge of dogs with her knowledge of being a mother. Never before has there been such a need for the information contained in these pages. With the recent bad publicity given to dogs, more and more mothers are becoming concerned about the relationship their dogs and their children.

As Silvia rightly points out, there really is no need to worry, providing the right kind of preparation, introduction and stress free training procedures have been carried out.

The emphasis throughout is on prevention. The guide encourages parents to anticipate problems and suggests ways of guarding against them. Where there already is a problem, her "Action Plans" will show parents how to overcome them.

None of the methods described involve any kind of physical confrontation with the dog - they are based upon the building of trust between the parent, the dog and the child or baby..

The major cause for concern is how to introduce a new baby into a household where there is already a resident dog.

Many perfectly well adjusted dogs have to go through the trauma of being rehomed and some are unfortunately put to sleep simply because the parents to be are unsure how the dog will react and are understandably not prepared to take any risks.

This guide will allay their fears and give them a positive programme to follow which will result in a succesful introduction and the formation of a long lasting bond.

As a canine behaviourist, I know that the subjects covered in this guide really do relate to the questions mothers and mothers to be want to know about, because they are the very questions most frequently asked of me.

Now that Silvia has collated them, I personally will find it extremely useful in my day to day practise of dealing with the problem behaviour of pet dogs, especially where young children are involved.

JOHN FISHER
FOUNDER MEMBER,
ASSOCIATION OF PET BEHAVIOUR CONSULTANTS

INTRODUCTION

Some of my fondest childhood memories relate to an old mongrel who belonged to my aunt. He was my playmate, my protector and my best friend; and he taught me about taking responsibility for a a fellow creature.

My children now have their own best friends - Alex aged nine has a German Shepherd Bitch called Rio who sleeps by his bed at night. Baby Stephen aged 10 months loves our White Miniature Poodle pup Sweep who can always cheer him up simply by walking into the room and staying close to him.

I cannot start to thank our dogs for all they have taught the children; be it patience, learning to see things from someone else's point of view, perseverance and self confidence, but most of all a realistic regard and esteem for animals a million miles away from the sickly sweet "little people in furry outfits" image they are subjected to every time they switch on the TV.

In owning and caring for a dog we experience first hand what it is like to be responsible for a small part of creation. And, just as owning a dog entails much more commitment, time and trouble than owning a goldfish or a hamster, the relationship we develop with our dog is correspondingly deeper and far more satisfying.

I firmly believe that dogs are good for people; and I know dogs can be good for children.

All it takes is a little foresight and some sympathetic guidance by the parent to create a worthwhile partnership which will become part of your own child's fondest memories in years to come.

Silvia Hartmann-Kent
September 1990

Chapter 1

Pregnancy, childbirth and what it's like to live with a baby are amongst those events you must have experienced yourself in order to understand what they are really like. However, the main factor in trying to prepare your family dog is to try and think ahead.

Try to imagine the demands that will be made on the dog and take steps well in advance, identifying and anticipating possible problem areas before they arise.

This is what this book is all about - preventing problems. It is also hoped that it will anwer the questions which tend to be raised when a new addition to the family is on the way. Do remember, most dogs adapt very happily to life in the new extended family and statistically only a minute percentage ever need specialist advice.

I hope you will find as you go through the sections that your own dog is already perfectly well prepared. If you are unsure, there is a quick Check List in Appendix II to help you put your mind at rest.

Should you already have a problem I hope you will find some guidelines towards a solution. All training methods involved are simple and do not involve physical confrontation; should you need any further expert help you will find some useful addresses in Appendix III.

Let us now begin by looking at an aspect of dog ownership which every member of the family will be involved in at one time or another - and it is simply about touching your dog.

HANDLING

Handling describes how a dog reacts to being touched by people he knows, be it during caretaking activities such as bathing, brushing etc., during training or simply as stroking or petting.

> *Peter and Julie were very concerned that their 3 year old Collie Luke might bite their new baby as he hated having his back end touched and would snap if anyone reached for his rear or his tail.*

Young babies and toddlers grab at things - we all know that. They also try to pull things into their mouths and suck or bite them.

It follows how important it is for the family dog to be happy about being touched and handled all over his body, as well as having his tail, ears and fur lightly pulled.

In order to teach a dog who does not like being handled, follow the first "Action Plan" overleaf; but even dogs who do not snap or react badly to being touched will benefit from the "Handling Action Plan" because

a. dogs enjoy it;
b. it is very relaxing for the owner;
c. it helps towards bonding;
d. it makes every day task such as bathing, grooming or treatments easier;
e. potential troubles such as fleas, grazes etc. are detected early before they can turn into a serious problem.

Basic Principles

Teaching your dog to enjoy being touched is in no way meant to be a struggle. Never go on to the next stage if your dog is not comfortable. Take your time. Never get upset and shout or punish - simply walk away and try again later if your dog won't co-operate to begin with.

Handling Action Plan

Step 1
Find a time when your dog is naturally relaxed - after a walk of after a meal.

Simply stroke his head and shoulders with firm, long, slow strokes and talk quietly to him. Do this until he is reaxed and happy to accept it quietly, without becoming excited, aggressive or playful.

This stage can take up to two weeks of twice daily sessions depending on your dog, but it is important to take your time. This exercise lays the foundations for all which follows.

Step 2
Only when your dog is happy with the above, sit on the floor with him. Extend the strokes, still starting from his head and shoulders, to his back and towards his chest.

Do not at this stage try to push on too quickly. Take it slowly and remember that you are trying to build your dog's confidence.

The aim of the exercise is a dog who is deeply relaxed and showing no signs of worry or apprehension.

IT IS GOOD FOR YOUR DOG TO KNOW THAT...

... AT LEAST SOME THINGS NEVER CHANGE!

Step 3

Very gradually over a period of 10 - 20 sessions extend the "stroking area" until you can touch every part of his body without him becoming unhappy or tense.

Step 4

Only then move to lightly holding his ears, paws and tail - only a touch at first, with a little more pressure each time to do this exercise. Should your dog show resentment or fear, back off and go back to the "safe areas" for time being.

Step 5

When you can firmly hold and stroke every part of his body start gently tugging on the fur on his chest - and I mean gently! Build this up gradually again as before until he is quite happy.

Step 6

Ask other people the dog knows well to pet and stroke him as often as possible. If your dog is not particularly keen on other people he can be persuaded to accept being handled by always receiving a small food treat after having been touched.

You yourself should continue to have one handling session with your dog at least once a day, even if you can only spare a couple of minutes.

Once the baby has been born, those few intimate moments you share with your dog will not be affected by your state of fitness and will serve to establish continuity in a world where everything else has changed.

Chapter 2
EXERCISE

If you are pregnant for the first time it is hard to look beyond the actual birth - the major event looming ahead. Furthermore, not many women really realise that even the easiest of births will make walking difficult, if not impossible, during the first two weeks at least. This is partially due to discomfort and partially due to bleeding which occurs naturally after each birth but which does require you to rest in order to facilitate proper healing.

> *Susan sought help because her 18 month old Labrador Lady had become very destructive since the birth of the baby. After talking for a while it transpired that Lady had been used to go for very long walks all through Susan's pregnancy. Susan had had a number of stitches she found walking now very uncomfortable and had not taken Lady out at all since the baby had been born. Lady was now exercised only briefly by the husband when he came home from work and used up her excess energy during the day by chewing.*

Even when you have fully recovered from child birth there will be further impediments to lengthy walks and games in the park with your dog.

> *Sheba, a German Shepherd Bitch, had developed a whole catalogue of problems during the last year. Continuous barking, stealing articles and refusing to give them up, not coming in from the garden when called and over excitable behaviour with visitors were amongst them. Sheba was hardly exercised at all as Mary just could not cope with*

the dog pulling on the lead and the pushchair at the
same time. When Mary went out, Sheba had to stay
at home.

Exercise does not, however, simply consist of walking the legs off your dog.

Dogs enjoy going out because they like walking, but because of the sights, the sounds, the smells and the expectation of what and whom they are going to meet. In fact there are dogs who hardly ever leave their owners house and yet live contented and happy lives because they are provided with interest and stimulation in other ways.

Talking to or playing with your dog, grooming it or training it can all provide interest in a dog's life if walks are in short supply.

Action Plan

1. It is as well to put well meaning friends and relatives to the test when they offer to take your dog out for you. Try it for a week and see how much exercise your dog is really going to get if you cannot take him out yourself.

2. Get your dog used to staying at home on occasion, especially if you feel like walking a lot during your pregnancy.

3. Most importantly, now's the time to teach your dog to heel on a loose lead. Once your baby has arrived, this task will be one hundred percent more difficult. If you 're unsure of how to do this, you can find a brief outline in the "Exercises" chapter.

4. Exercise also includes keeping a dog's mind exercised. Simple obedience exercises, tricks and games can all be employed to keep a dog happy and relaxed even when it does not go out for long walks every day. See "Tricks & Games" in Appendix I for some ideas on the subject.

5. Teach your dog to retrieve articles. This will enable you to stay in one place whilst the dog does all the running and can be very useful to provide both physical exercise as well as mental stimulation indoors or in the garden.

6. Consider joining a dog training club, even if your dog is very obedient already. You can find advertisements for classes on your vetenary surgeon's notice board or in pet shop windows. Visit all the clubs in your area before you decide which one to join; look for a club with a happy, quiet atmosphere, relaxed looking dogs and friendly instructors.

Going to classes together once a week can be a welcome break from your normal every day routine for both you and your dog and it will be a chance to spend some time together without any distractions.

MANY DOGS HEARTILY DISLIKE BABIES NEAR THEIR BOWL.

Chapter 3
FOOD

Some dogs can take a pretty dim view of a toddler crawling towards their bowl whilst they are having their dinner, or having a favourite bone taken away and sucked.

A large percentage of accidents occur in situations involving food, so it is important that your dog should learn not to guard his bowl and bone, and to take food treats gently.

Action Plan

1. Feed your dog twice a day to keep his blood sugar levels fairly evenly distributed. This will make your dog less likely to be starving hungry.

2. Do not leave uneaten dog food lying around. Get your dog used to eating his food straight away by putting the bowl down, setting an egg timer to five minutes and immediately removing the food when the time is up. Harden your heart and do not offer the food again until at least six hours later.

3. Train your dog to be "baby safe". The trick is to teach your dog that it is "Good News" indeed when humans approach the bowl. Rather than marching up to the dog in a very aggressive manner and tearing the bowl from under it's nose ("to teach it who's boss"), wait until all the food has been eaten - then add a particularly tasty treat to the bowl.Within a very short period of time your dog will be eating and looking at you at the same time, virtually willing you to put your hand in his bowl. You can then progress to picking the bowl off the ground before adding the tread, then giving it back.

4. Try to ask friends and visitors to put the odd treat into your dog's bowl at any time of day. If you can, have some visiting children do the same; they will enjoy this and so will your dog!

5. Practise taking your dog's bone or chew away from him in the same positive way as you taught him to enjoy your hand near his bowl. Exchange the bone/chew for a particularly tasty treat, then give it back straight away, praising your dog as you do so.

6. Teach your dog to take food treats nicely and without snapping. This is best done in the evening after your dog's main meal to begin with. Treat it as a regular practise "exercise" - your dog is bound to enjoy it.

7. Sit on the floor with your dog and a biscuit. Teach him not to touch it unless you have specifically allowed him to do so. You will find this comes in handy when your baby starts learning to eat rusks on his own.

Chapter 4
TOYS

Toys can cause a lot of problems. Up to the arrival of the baby the only toys around the house will have belonged to the dog, so it is only natural that he assumes all the baby's toys must belong to him as well.

The fact that the baby's toys will also lie on the floor and are usually made of similar materials does not of course help to lessen the dog's confusion.

> *Micky, a Jack Russell Terrier, was in the doghouse for systematically shredding all baby Simon's toys. Simon's mother was getting worried because Micky would now growl at the eight month old boy and snatch toys from his hands.*
>
> *His owners could not understand why Micky did this as he had lots of toys of his own - in fact Micky's toy box was just as well stocked as Simon's.*

To avoid toy problems. take the following steps.

Action Plan

1. Limit the number of toys the dog can play with to one or two favourite articles. There really is no need for more, unless your dog is a very young puppy and still teething.

2. Practise taking toys away from your dog by exchanging them

for a food treat and praising sincerely, then giving them back straight away.

Under no circumstances should you adopt an aggressive stance when you do this - your dog might let you get away with it, but he most certainly would not back down from a little baby.

Remember you are trying to teach the dog to actually look forward to someone approaching him and his toy and to give him confidence that there's no need to guard his possessions.

3. Buy some fairly cheap perfume and use this as a marker for objects your dog is not allowed to touch. A very light spraying with the perfume from a fair distance (a foot or more) is quite enough - the scent will stand out like a torch to a dog's sensitive nose. An object to practise with could be a new furry toy or just a piece of cloth, for example.

Practise this when you are at ease and have time to see that the dog leaves the marked object alone. Start by placing it in a position where the dog is not likely to pick it up, then leaving it on chairs or low tables before finally moving it to the floor.

Remember to put the article away when you have finished the training session; if your dog gets hold of it and has a chance to play with it or chew it, the wrong lesson is learned!

Poppy, a cross breed, was crazy about squeaky toys. The slightest squeak would send her barking, jumping and generally going crazy with excitement. Her owner Pat was at her wit's end and worried that Poppy would inadvertantly hurt the baby, as there were squeaks in little Daniel's playgym, his Activity Bear, his shape sorter, his teddy and even in some of his rattles.

It is very common for dogs to take a particular sound as an excuse to go wild with excitement. The rattle of car keys, the sound of the lead being moved, the ringing of the telephone, the sound of the door bell, a squeaky toy as in Poppy's case and a whole host of others.

The owner's natural reaction to this is to try and avoid making the particular sound in order to stop the dog from becoming overexcited. But this approach is not a cure and usually serves to make the problem worse and worse.

All of the sounds above have in common that they only occur just before something exciting is going to take place - a game, a walk, the arrival of a visitor, mum dropping everything and rushing headlong for the telephone etc.

These sort of problems can be cured quite simply by making the sounds randomly a number of times - but without anything happening at all.

In Poppy's case her owner was advised to squeak the toy lots of times whilst ignoring the dog.

Initially Poppy went mad with excitement each time but she soon calmed down and lost interest in the sound, only becoming excited about the toy when she was actually allowed to play with it - and little Daniel could at last play with his Fisher Price Activity Centre in peace.

Chapter 5
SLEEPING PLACES

Beds, baskets, hidey holes and sleeping places in general can cause problems, especially when a dog feels the need to protect them from the human members of his family.

Unfortunately, dogs and babies tend to find the same kind of enclosed spaces attractive which can make the situation worse.

> *Ria, a small Terrier Cross, was very tolerant of the three young children in the household - but not when she had taken up residence under the coffee table in the sitting room.*
>
> *Ria would snarl and snap at anything that tried to enter her "den" and her owner Cindy was getting increasingly concerned about her possibly biting one of the children who seemed to make a beeline for the table and Ria every time her back was turned.*

Every dog deserves a "safe place" to which he can retire when the going gets rough - preferably in a quiet room not accessible to the child or children.

Such a "safe place' is not only good for the dog but can also be a real help to the owners as well as it is often much less stressful for everyone concerned to send the dog to his bed rather than to have to command and reprimand him constantly.

An indoor kennel or a crate (the civilised word for a cage) can provide an ideal retreat for your dog. Dogs usually enjoy staying in this kind of "den" providing they have been taught initially that it is a good place to be in (see "Crate Training in Appendix I).

A family dog must not however feel the need to protect his sleeping places from familiar human beings - with young babies or toddlers around this could lead to very unpleasant situations.

General Principles

As before, do not take an aggressive stance when trying to train a dog who guards his sleeping places.

Aggression always breeds aggression, and although you as an adult might force the dog into submission, it will not stand for such treatment from the baby.

The basic principle is again to teach the dog to think that if someone approaches his sleeping place he can anticipate good things happening, as opposed to him cringing back in anticipation of a fight or a struggle.

Action Plan

1. Set up a "safe place" for your dog and get him used to going to it and staying in it (see "Go To Bed!" and "Crate Training" in Appendix I).

2. If your dog likes to "guard" special places such as behind the settee, under a table, in a favourite chair for example, block off, remove or fill in these troublespots for time being until your dog has become accustomed to using his new retreat instead.

3. Approach your dog in his new retreat in a friendly manner, stroke and pat him, praise him and give him an occasional treat.

Should your dog be very much on guard and growl at you if you get too close, you could start by keeping a safe distance to begin with and to roll food treats towards him. Slowly decrease the distance until you are near enough to begin the above.

4. On occasion sit or stand in your dog's bed - and watch for the look of sheer amazement on your dog's face when you do this for the first time!

Invite him to join you and have a cuddle; this way your dog will feel quite relaxed when your baby eventually discovers his basket.

Sleeping Arrangements

One question you should also ask yourself is: Where does my dog sleep at the moment, and do I intend to change this once the baby has been born?

Gerry, a Spaniel, had started to mess indoors. He was five years old and had been perfectly house trained before the birth of the baby.

When I asked about sleeping arrangements it turned out that Gerry had slept in the bedroom right up until the baby had arrived. He now slept in the kitchen and was no longer allowed upstairs at all. He was not allowed in the dining room anymore and the furniture in the sitting room had also become out of bounds to him.

While we were talking he tried to climb onto the sofa and was pushed off by his owner with the words, "Get off! Baby doesn't want your hairs all over her settee!".

If your dog sleeps with you in the bedroom or on the bed and you do not wish to continue with this arrangement once the baby has been born, be sure to make all the necessary changes well in advance.

The same applies to the question whether or not the dog is allowed on the furniture. This is purely a matter of personal preference and only you can decide one way or the other, but the point is to be aware of how your dog will feel.

There will be many changes in your household due to the baby and for your dog this can be very frightening indeed.

Dogs need routines because they give them a feeling of security and of what to expect next in the bewildering world in which we humans live.

Changing a dog's routine sleeping place is an important issue to him and should therefore be firmly resolved whilst everything else is still comparatively normal.

Getting your dog accustomed to his new routine in advance will not only help him to adjust to the new situation more smoothly but will also make life easier for you too. It will be one little thing less on your mind and most importantly, your dog will not be able to connect the new routine with the arrival of the baby in any way.

Chapter 6
JEALOUSY & ATTENTION

With the best will in the world, your dog will not receive the same amount of attention from you after the baby has been born.

Most dogs adapt to this change, but the transition can be made much smoother by a little foresight.

If you've never had a baby before, it comes as a shock to discover just how much time it will take up - every bit there is and sometimes more.

Think about it. Even if your baby behaves strictly according to schedule - and only about one in every hundred do - you will have to feed, burp, wash, change, dress and rock to sleep your baby every four hours. And when you're not directly engaged in these routine caretaking activities, you'll still be wanting some time just to hold, look at and cuddle your baby. And when it's finally gone to sleep, you'll be popping in every so often to check on its well being.

In fact we women are biologically programmed to have the baby on our mind continuously, at least for a period of time.

Even that is not all. People will be visiting to see the baby; midwives and health visitors popping in and out; there's all the extra house work the baby inevitably creates; you might want to give extra attention to your spouse so that he doesn't feel left out. Add to this that you most certainly won't feel very energetic at the time it becomes very obvious that a different world has arrived for your dog right out of the blue.

Your main concern therefore must be to lessen the difference between the "before" and "after" to some extent.

Action Plan
Before the birth:

1. Avoid focusing too much of your loving energy on your pet dog, especially towards the latter stages of pregnancy when time can seem to pass excrutiatingly slowly.

For your dog's sake, find someone else to talk to on occasion or leave him behind when you go out.

2. Teach your dog that there could be times when he is not required. To test his response, sit on the sofa, cuddle a cushion and talk lovingly to it.

Will he try to push in, claw at you, bring toys to get your attention? Now's the time to teach him to back off - so when the baby arrives, he can't blame it for the sudden change in your behaviour.

3. If you are always the one to feed, groom, train and exercise your dog, get someone else to do these things for you on occasion. This will prepare your dog for the time you might have to spend in hospital, and on your return home, when you're not allowed downstairs yet.

4. Generally prepare your dog for the possibility of an overall, albeit temporary, lack of attention. Examples of this would include to change your dog's diet temporarily to a canned or dried product if you usually cook elaborate meals for him, to have his fur cut short to eliminate the need for daily grooming, or to gradually reduce the length and frequency of walks and outings.

After the birth:

The first meeting

It is quite possible you will feel apprehensive when your dog first meets your new baby. You might wonder if your dog will like the baby.

Dogs on the whole have ho opinion at all about the baby yet - but they will be watching you for clues what opinion they ought to have.

If you are nervous and tense, the dog is likely to be the same and become suspicious of that strange new creature on your lap.

Ideally, be cheerful and loving towards the dog and let it have a good sniff. Most dogs will not actually lick the baby, just put their noses very close without touching. If the dog should lick the baby, don't worry, it is not be the end of the world (see "Hygiene").

If you are worried the dog might jump on the baby, place the baby in someone else's arms or on the sofa and kneel by your dog's side, holding the collar firmly but gently.

Say things like: "This is my own puppy, do you like it? Doesn't it look funny?", etc. etc. Your voice will automatically become soft and loving as you talk about the baby and to your dog this will sound like praise - the ideal setting.

This also works the other way around; when you are holding the baby, talk to the baby about the dog: "Look baby, here is Fido. He is a **good dog**. He's going to help me look after you." etc. etc.

Again your dog is being praised in the baby's presence which is an excellent start to their future relationship.

37

If your dog shows no interest in the baby at all and looks away or just pays attention to you, still procede as above and talk to him in a loving way about the baby. It is vital at this early stage that your dog should learn to think along the lines of "When this new creature is around, I get praised. Therefore I like having it around."

The first few weeks

Bruno, a Doberman, had been alright with the baby at first. Now, 4 weeks later, he was beginning to show signs of aggression towards the baby, giving it "dirty looks" as the husband termed it and growling at it when he was close by.

When I saw this family there was an air of great strain and unhappiness about them, both husband and wife repeatedly shouting at the dog and pushing him away when he got too close to the baby. Eventually the wife took the baby away. As soon as they had left the room, the husband relaxed visibly, starting to stroke the dog and to talk soothingly to him.

As far as Bruno was concerned, it could always be like this - if only he could get rid of the baby ...

Action Plan

1. Try to avoid shouting, pushing, smacking etc. your dog when the baby is near at all cost. Use positive commands such as "Sit" or "Down" rather than negative commands such as "Leave" or "Off" so your dog knows what you want him to do and you can praise him for obeying.

If your dog is very boisterous and won't leave you or your baby alone you can attach a length of line to the dog's collar and tie it up close to you. A small dog can be controlled in this way by just wrapping the line around your foot. Both these methods control the dog's behaviour effectively - but without you personally becoming unpleasant towards the dog.

2. Do not fall into the trap of "trying to make it up to the dog" by giving him a lot of extra attention (i.e. fussing him or playing with him) when the baby has gone to bed.

This will be interpreted by the dog - just as Bruno did in the last example - like this: "When the baby is here, they ignore me. When it is not here, I'm having a wonderful time. Therefore I don't like the baby."

Ideally you should sometimes pay attention to the dog when the baby is present, and sometimes ignore him when the baby is not present.

If you have a jealousy problem already, always ignore the dog when the baby is away and only pay attention when the baby is around (even asleep in a push chair will do).

3. Make a point of praising your dog occasionally when he's doing nothing in particular, sleeping in his basket or amusing himself quietly on his own for example.

It often happens that a dog will only receive attention when he's being "naughty" if his owners are busy or preoccupied - and you will be both just after the birth of your baby. The result is of course that the dog will be "naughty" more and more often to remind you of his existence.

A quick pat or a cuddle and a few kind words to your dog at the right time is an easy way of reassuring him that you have not forgotten him and to avoid attention related behaviour problems.

WHAT'S WHAT, OFTEN DEPENDS ENTIRELY ON YOUR
POINT OF VIEW!

*Kim, a Samoyed, was driving her owner Michelle
to distraction by barking, rushing around and a
number of other activities when Michelle tried to
feed the baby.*

*Orders and commands would not stop her and
when Michelle tried shutting Kim in the kitchen she
howled like a wolf and scratched madly at the door
- which made feeding times extremely stressful for
Michelle.*

Be aware of "attention getting behaviour" by the dog - it can take
all kinds of bizarre forms.

Favourites are barking, whining, scratching at the door to be let
out into the garden, picking up an object and challenging you to a
"catch me if you can" session but there are countless others -
chasing shadows, chasing the tail, snapping at imaginary flies,
pretending a visitor has arrived; the list is really quite endless and
only limited by a dog's ingenuity.

**If you try to punish this kind of behaviour by shouting at your
dog, telling him to stop, chasing him etc. you have in fact
rewarded him, because he managed to gain your attention,
which is what he wanted in the first place.**

As far as a dog is concerned, negative attention (what we might
think of a s punishment) is much, much better than no attention at
all. Some dogs will even go so far as to prefer a beating to being
ignored.

The best way to cure problems relating to this and more
importantly, to curb them before they get out of hand as in Kim's
and Michelle's case, is to ignore the dog completely as soon as he
starts and to reward him by looking at him and praising him when
he has stopped.

Ignoring your dog when he's playing you up...

... and rewarding him when he's good...

... is easy and effective !

Chapter 7
HYGIENE

Hygiene is an interesting and emotionally charged area as opinions are deeple divided amongst experts on how much of a health hazard dogs really are, depending on which side of the fence they're on.

On the whole, people who do not own dogs will advise you that there are enormous risks in mixing dogs and babies.

Experts who are dog owners themselves, on the other hand, believe that the risks are minimal, providing some fairly basic rules of hygiene are observed.

Try to find a health visitor or midwife who actually owns a dog if you want to discuss the subject in more detail. Alternatively, talk to your vetenary surgeon - the ultimate expert on "dog borne diseases".

Please note that all the points in this chapter apply to normal, healthy children. Should your baby be premature or ill you might have to take stricter precautions. Discuss this with any of the above, if necessary.

General Points
As far as transmitting disease or illness is concerned, the basic rule is:

The cleaner and healthier the dog, the smaller the risk.

Most diseases transmitted by dogs to humans are caused by parasites such as worms (like the much publicised Toxocara Canis) or fleas or mites, which means if your dog does not have any worms, fleas or mites, it cannot transmit said diseases.

Dog hair is unsightly but unless ingested in large quantities is unlikely to cause any degree of harm to a healthy baby.

Dog saliva does carry large amounts of bacteria; for this reason it is vital that saliva should not get into open wounds. Any dog bite even if inflicted accidentally whilst playing should be cleaned professionally at your local hospital to avoid long lasting and painful infection. Normal healthy skin however will not suffer from occasional contact with it.

Any doggy "accidents" around the house should be cleaned and disinfected with specialist materials available from your vetenary surgeon as they are both stronger and longer lasting than those available from your supermarket or pet shop.

Action Plan

1. Start worming your dog at 3 monthly intervals before the baby is born and continue to do so regularly afterwards. Please make sure you enter the dates when you should be worming your dog in your diary and get an ample supply of tablets from your vetenary surgeon; it is only too easy to forget if you are busy.

Your vetenary surgeon will advise you on what kind of tablets and the dosage you need for your dog,

2. Make an effort to get rid of fleas. Fleas can carry diseases which could be introduced directily into the baby's bloodstream; you will have to treat not only the dog but also his bedding and your carpets, too. In England some councils provide a service to fumigate your house free of charge. Contact your local Town Hall and ask for the Department of Environmental Health, if you feel this to be necessary.

As before, your vetenary surgeon will be able to supply you with sprays or powders which are more powerful than those available elsewhere.

For preventing re-infestation you might consider a flea collar. A carpet freshner-cum-insecticide can also be of use but watch out for a possibility of allergic reactions to this from any human or animal members of your household.

3. Keep your dog clean and consider having his fur cut short by a professional groomer before the baby is born. Don't worry how it looks; it will save you a lot of time to begin with and you can soon go back to the more glamorous hair style when the baby is a little older.

4. Keep your dog's annual injections up to date. One of the diseases your dog will be protected from can be transmitted to humans (Leptospirosis or Weil's Disease) and can be fatal.

5. Be sensible and do not use the baby's dishes for dog food and vice versa.

6. Keep some antiseptic soap around for washing your hands after cleaning up after your dog, feeding him or after bathing him when he's rolled in something objectionable.

On the whole, however, trying to wash your hands every time you've touched the dog or anything that has been touched by the dog will probably drive you mad if he lives in the house with you. It is not at all necessary unless you, your dog or your baby are ill.

Discuss this further with your vetenary surgeon, if necessary.

7. If your feed fresh or frozen meats intended for animal consumption be careful where you store them and keep all implements used strictly apart from your other kitchenware. Always scrub your hands thoroughly after handling them.

Proprietary canned, dried or semi moist dog foods on the other hand have been cooked and sterilised at great length and do not pose a health hazard any more than an ordinary can of stewed steak unless allowed to go off.

Chapter 8
PHYSICAL SAFETY

When we talk about physical safety with regards to dogs the first thing that springs to mind is injury through dog bites.

With the recent media coverage one could be forgiven to think that "attacks" by houselhold pets on their owners and children are a commonplace occurence.

Fortunately this is not so. For ever reported incident there are literally tens of thousands of happy, well adjusted family dogs who never put a paw wrong.

It is as well though to be aware of possibly dangerous situations and to take sensible precautions.

I. Accidental Biting

A recent survey shows that 93% of all reported incidents of bites relate to dogs that have never bitten anyone before.

What this simple statistic means is there are thousands of owners who, right up until 2 seconds before the actual incident, would have sworn blind that **their** dog was "absolutely trustworthy".

Now I love dogs dearly. I work with them and own a large number myself - but I would never describe any dog as absolutely trustworthy - for what does "trustworthy" actually mean?

MISUNDERSTANDING, RATHER THAN BAD INTENT,
IS USUALLY THE CAUSE OF ALL EVIL.

Carry, a seven year old mongrel, had bitten 18 months old Jason in the shoulder. The little boy needed over thirty stitches and while he was being treated in hospital the dog was taken to be destroyed.

When the vetenary surgeon's assistant was about to remove the body from the table, she noticed something in the dog's ear. It was a pencil stub that had penetrated Carry's ear drum.

A dog might be thoroughly good natured and "trustworthy" around children, but unsupervised children should never, ever be trusted around a dog.

Take heed, be aware of your responsibilities to your child and your dog and take some common sense precautions.

Action Plan

1. Invest in a sturdy playpen while your baby is still very small. The wooden "cage" type is the best, but if your dog is small you might have to choose the "lobsterpot" type to prevent him from getting in through the bars.

A playpen is a must for every mother, let alone dog owners, to ensure the child's (and the dog's!) safety when you have to leave the room to answer the telephone or the door, make coffee etc.

2. Later on, safety gates can be used to seperate more active children from the dog when you are not in the same room to supervise.

Buy the type that have a little door in them as we do not want to encourage the dog to jump the safety gates.

3. Set up a retreat for your dog in a quiet room preferably not accessible to the child. This can be a real life saver when you have visitors with children, during birthday parties or simply when you are too busy to supervise.

Note the word is "retreat" and not "solitary confinement"; get the dog used to the place (such as an indoor kennel, crate or basket) very gradually until he looks forward to staying in it. See also "Sleeping Places", "Crate Training" and "Go to Bed" for further information. If at all possible the dog should be used to going to his retreat before the birth so he does not connect being sent away by you with the arrival of the baby.

4. Keep an eye on your dog's general state of health at all times. Physical problems leading to sore or sensitive areas are the most common reason for a dog biting or snapping when touched.

A very common example of this is a dislike to be touched near the tail due to impacted anal glands; ear infections are often the reason for a dog reacting badly to be handled near his head or neck.

II. Non-accidental Biting

A rather different situation arises when the dog bites not for immediate physical reasons as in the above examples, but when guarding or protecting his possesions or favourite sleeping places.

> *Khan, a Great Dane, had snapped at the young child in the family shortly after it had started to crawl. There had been no damage but his owners were shocked and deeply worried and were thinking of having him destroyed.*
>
> *It transpired during the course of the interview that Khan had always guarded his toys, bed and bowl from both the husband and the wife ever since he was a puppy.*

Every dog should have a place he can retire to—
when the going gets rough!

Although Khan's owners described his "attack" as surprising and shocking, all the signs had been there long before the baby ever arrived.

Khan was simply exercising his rights as a "pack leader" to tell the baby off for encroaching on his possessions. He had also given all the warnings beforehand that would have been required from a normal, healthy dog when dealing with members of his own family.

The stages of a dog's warning are often overlooked and it is usually only with hindsight that the owners realise that the eventual bite was an inevitable escalation.

These are the stages:

1. The dog stops what he is doing and becomes very still.

2. If this is ignored, the dog will look threateningly directly at the intruder.

3. If the intruder still persists, the dog will flatten his ears and may growl.

4. Then he will lift his lip and growl more loudly.

5. Only then will the dog snap out, not to injure, but to teach the intruder a lesson.

When a dog deals with puppies, one snap is usually enough to teach the pup to respect the other warnings.

Human "puppies" however are not programmed to understand this system and a dog will feel he has to resort to going straight into the "punishment stage" after his low level warnings have been repeatedly ignored.

There again, a snap that would only bruise a puppy through its thick skin and protective fur could seriously injure a human child.

Khan was not an aggressive or dangerous dog. His owners had to make the choice whether they were going to re-train him or have him put to sleep - when all the problems could have been avoided with a little foresight.

Action Plan

1. Look at your dog realistically and identify all possible problem areas. Use the "Check List" in Appendix II and answer the questions truthfully.

If you are even slightly unsure about any of the questions, refer to the related Action Plans and start practising straight away, so your dog is safe before your baby arrives.

2. Under no circumstance must you adopt an aggressive "me master, you dog" approach. Your dog might well bow to your pressure under threat of punishment - but this is not going to make him safe with your baby.

Only by positive, reward based training as outlined in the "Action Plans" can you ensure your dog will be happy to accept your little human near his toys, basket, bowl, etc.

Should you yourself have any problems like the above with your dog you might well have what is called a "dominance" problem. This means basically that your dog considers himself to be higher ranking than you and will feel justified to make his own decisions on occasion and to be prepared to defend them from you.

Women (and believe me, I hate to have to say this!) can have problems establishing dominance, especially over male dogs.

This can be further exacerbated during pregnancy and whilst breast feeding by the abundance of female hormons in your system. Their presence can be picked up by a dog on your scent and the result is that in the dog's eyes you have become a "super female" - to be loved and protected, but not necessarily to be obeyed!

A good dog behaviour consultant can point you in the right direction to correct dominance related problems (see Appendix III for address).

One word of warning: Should anyone, no matter how expert he or she purports to be, advise you to use methods based on physical punishment such as hitting, shaking, choking, spraying unpleasant substances, using sound deterrants or shock collars, thank them politely and show them the door immediately.

Methods based on physical punishment are totally unsuitable for your situation and can be very dangerous indeed when employed in the context of training a dog to be safe with babies and children.

III. General Safety

Injury to children can occur as the result of a boisterous greeting as an unsteady toddler can easily be knocked over; being caught accidentally by claws is another common cause of injury.

Safety in the car is another area you should be considering; as in all the other Action Plans, now's the time to teach the dog to behave in a civilised fashion to avoid causing accidents.

Action Plan

1. Teach your dog to greet in a civilised manner without jumping up. If you're not sure how to do this you can find some tips on the subject under "Exercises" in Appendix I.

2. Do discourage any jumping up, anytime. Try to convince your partner or anyone else in regular contact with your dog of the necessity to do this with regards to your toddler-to-be. (If you have a particular reason to want your dog to jump up at you, working in competitive obedience for example, teach the dog only to jump when the appropriate signal has been given and discourage at any other time).

3. Run with your dog, waving your arms and shouting "Yipee!" to test how strong his chasing instincts are (and take no notice of what the neighbaurs might make of that!). Many dogs get very excited by this kind of behaviour and react by jumping up, snapping at your ankles or trying to grab hold of you with their teeth.

Should your dog react in this fashion, put him on a lead and teach him to run with you without jumping or snapping. Keep practising

TEST YOUR DOG'S CHASING INSTINCT—
AND NEVER MIND THE NEIGHBAURS!

this on the odd occasion and when your baby has become an active two year old, you will be glad you did.

4. In the car some kind of restraint is a must and you should fit a dog guard if at all possible. A dog leaping onto a baby in its carrycot or car seat can not only cause injury, but also distract the driver and thereby causing an accident.

If you cannot fit a dog guard you might consider a nylon harness which acts as a seat belt for your dog instead. A cheaper but less satisfactory way of restraining a dog in the car is to tie the dog using a leather collar (**not** a check chain or half check!) and a lead.

Whichever restraining method in the car you opt for, start using it straight away to get the dog and yourself used to the procedure well in advance.

Chapter 9
TRAINING YOUR BABY

So far we have only been concerned with child proofing the dog. But as it usually takes "two to tango", the child will also have to learn how to behave in an acceptable fashion towards the dog.

> *Sharon was seriously considering having her dog Elsa, a five year old Golden Retriever, put to sleep as the dog was apparently getting less and less tolerant of the two boys aged 2 and 4.*
>
> *During the interview both boys smacked Elsa repeatedly, pulled her tail, threw toys at her and sat on her. None of this behaviour elicited any comment whatsoever from Sharon. Finally Elsa growled as one of the boys tried to climb on her back.*
>
> *Sharon jumped up in mid sentence, hit the dog around the face and dragged her from the room. On her return she said triumphantly, "Now do you see what problems I have?"*

If things go wrong it is often the dog who has to take all the blame.

Babies and young children are driven by the need to explore and cannot be expected to know or realise what consequences their actions might have.

Having said that, it is never too early to point your baby in the right direction, using - just as you did with your dog - encouragement and praise rather than shouting or punishment.

Action Plan

1. First and foremost be realistic and do not expect too much of a small child - they really have no idea of how other creatures feel and very little control over their strength or movements.

2. From a very early age hold your baby's hand and make him stroke the dog slowly and gently, saying "Nice doggie, nice doggie" at the same time.

Should the baby try to grab, straighten out his fingers for him and say something like, "Like this, sweetheart, Nice doggie."

3. When your baby gets a little older and can move about by himself, do not let him pester the dog. Let him go up to your "child proofed" dog by all means but distract the baby away if you feel your dog has had enough.

This is only fair to your canine companion and will start to build good habits for your baby.

4. If you follow this theme right from the start, you will never have "the sort of problem" Sharon experienced in the last example.

Encourage friendly attention from your child towards the dog within reason at all times.

Should your child later try to behave in a way one could regard as unfair on the dog, tell him firmly that you are not happy and will not stand for this kind of behaviour.

5. Encourage your child from a very early age to take part in the every day care of your family dog.

Even a very young child can "help" with brushing, feeding, bathing and even training the dog - you will find that both dogs and children love this and their relationship will benefit greatly from it.

Chapter 10
DECISIONS

You have read through the book and completed the "Check List". If you have found that your dog is well adjusted and perfectly happy I hope your mind is now at rest and all is well in your household.

It would be unrealistic and naive to assume, however, that is is going to be the case for everyone.

Perhaps a dog is very old or ill. Perhaps it is a rescued dog with numerous problems in his past. Perhaps circumstances - where you live, whether you are well, financial problems - are against you.

In these cases a decision will have to be made. Should you keep your dog, and if not, what is to become of him?

I am often asked to advise whether a dog should be kept or not. Neither I nor any other person can make this kind of decision for you. All I can do is give you all the facts, for the final decision and the final responsibility lies with you alone.

Options
The very fact that you have gone to the trouble of buying and reading this book shows that you are a caring owner who shudders at the kind of mentality that makes some people simply dump a dog by the side of a motorway.

If the decision has been made that it is not possible to keep the dog, there are basically two options available.

You can either try to find a new home for your dog, or you can have him put to sleep.

Which one of these options you choose must depend on the dog and whether or not you believe that he would make a good pet for someone else.

Let us now look at both in more detail and see what they entail.

Finding a new home

The "big farm in the country" where a retired couple without children is going to look after the dog all day is what many people like to believe their dog will go to.

It is unfortunately a myth. Many, many more dogs are looking for homes than there are homes looking for dogs.

Even so, a proportion of "second hand dogs" find new owners eventually. There are a number of organisations which might help you find a new home for your dog, or you could re-home your dog yourself.

Rescue Shelters
The most usual cause of action is to take the dog to a rescue society such as the RSPCA or a local private shelter.

Although this is a possibility, please bear in mind that shelters are generally overcrowded and desperately short of funds; by taking your dog you will add to their burden. You must also be aware that you will be giving up all control over what is going to happen to the dog once you signed your name on the dotted line.

If you are going to give up your dog to a shelter, enquire first for how long they will keep the dog as this can vary from a minimum of seven days up to however long it takes to find a new owner.

Breed Rescue Organisations
If your dog is a pedigree dog, you might find there is a specialist rescue organisations just for your breed.

These are run locally and nationwide and are staffed by dedicated breed enthusiasts who can be most experienced and helpful. Generally breed rescue organisations do not run kennels themselves and prefer the dog to stay with you until a new owner has been found although they will endeavour to find somewhere for your dog to stay at short notice in an emergency.

Finding a new home yourself
If you have the time, this is probably the most satisfactory way of re-homing your dog. Begin by advertising in your local newspaper, placing cards in pet shop windows and news agent's notice boards. Dog training clubs, dog wardens and vetenary surgeons can also be of help.

Please be very truthful about any possible "vices" your dog might have. If someone is put off by what he hears he would not have been the right person for your dog in any case and the dog might have been returned to you with some new problems added at a later date.

Get to know the prospective new owner; let the dog stay with them for a day, then a weekend before making the final move. This is much less traumatising to both you and your dog and the very best way to make a painful transition as easy as possible.

Putting the dog to sleep

Sometimes this can be the only option left to the owner and a more difficult and heartbreaking decision is hard to imagine.

In certain cases however it is the right decision and the only responsible thing to do.

> *Joan was faced with this decision. Her dog Minnie, a poodle, was 16 years old and had been with Joan since she had been a child. Minnie was blind, partly deaf and required a lot of special care as she also suffered from incontinence.*
>
> *"I took her to the surgery. It was the hardest thing I've ever had to do in my life. Looking back on it, I realise that I did the right thing. Minnie needed so much attention which I wouldn't have been able to give her and she would not have understood what was going on. Really, the arrival of the baby just forced me to make a decision I perhaps should have made a long time ago."*

Your vetenary surgeon will probably enquire into your reasons why you wish your dog to be put down and will be kind and sympathetic. You might be asked whether you want to take the body home for burial. It is best to make all the necessary arrangements, including paying the fee, well in advance to make the whole procedure less distressing.

You can stay with your dog if you like, or you can take him to the surgery and leave.

The actual process is kind and totally pain free. The dog is injected intravenously with a concentrated barbiturate which works so quickly that it is sometimes hard to believe the dog is indeed dead. He is literally put to sleep.

Appendix I

EXERCISES

Training Your Dog

Basic Principles
Whatever you want to teach your dog, be it simple obedience exercises or complex tricks, follow these basic rules.

1. Try to stand back a little from your normal relationship with your dog; be a teacher rather than a concerned mum. I assure you it helps!

2. Be very clear what exactly you want your dog to do and how you are going to teach it before you start.

3. Always approach your training from a positive angle and teach the dog what you want it to do, as opposed to trying to teach the dog to stop something or not to do something. Examples are teaching your dog to sit still rather than to try and teach it to "stop jumping", teaching your dog to walk by your side rather than to try and teach it to "stop pulling" etc.

4. Break each exercise into small and manageable components and teach only one step at a time. This makes learning and teaching easier and it is how all professionals work and how television and film animals are taught to perform their marvellous tricks.

5. Never train your dog when you are not feeling well and should you become angry or frustrated during a session, stop straight away.

6. Remember that your dog is an animal and not a person in a furry outfit. Always give your dog the benefit of the doubt if he doesn't respond straight away and resort to more training rather than to punishment.

7. Dog training is like dieting. In order to get results you have to be strong willed and must persevere.

Trying something a couple of times and then giving up on the grounds that it didn't work is a sure fire road to failure.

Results will always be directly proportional to the amount of effort you are prepared to put in.

Walking to Heel

Step 1.

Start off with your dog siting quietly by your left hand side and looking at you.

Take your time because if your dog cannot manage to do this, you have no chance to make him heel once you are moving. Holding a piece of food in your hand can help get the dog's attention before you start.

Step 2.

Say your dog's name and "Heel" clearly while the dog is looking at you to make sure he's heard the command. Step off and walk a very tight left hand circle with your dog on the inside, using your body and your legs to keep the dog back rather than pulling on the lead.

When you have reached your starting point, put the dog into a "Sit" by your side and reward and praise it, regardless of whether he did well or not. Have your lead very, very loose as the dog will automatically pull against it if it is tight (pushme-pullyou effect).

Practise small left hand circles until your dog anticipates your moves and no longer tries to push into you.

Step 3.

Using the same sequence as above, walk different patterns such as ovals, right handed circles, fig. 8's and straight lines. If your dog gets in front of you, walk straight into a very tight left turn and go back to the circle in Step 2.

Always start from a "Sit" with full attention, always end in a "Sit"

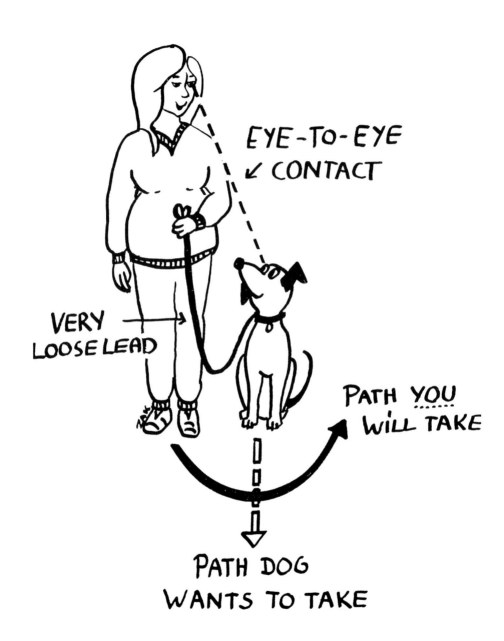

EYE-TO-EYE
↙ CONTACT

VERY
LOOSE LEAD

PATH YOU
WILL TAKE

PATH DOG
WANTS TO TAKE

with lots of praise.

Step 4.
This is the most important part of the training, as your command to heel must now become an "absolute" for the dog.

If you give the command and the dog begins to get in front of you, stop immediately, tell the dog you are disgusted, take it backwards to beyond the starting point and put it back into the sit, ready to start all over again.

I realise that even the shortest walk can take a very long time, as you are stopping and walking backwards constantly; it is important at this stage however that your dog learns you will do something to back up your command once it has been given.

From a practical point of view, there will be times when you just have not got the time to enforce your heel command each time. If this should happen, **do not give any command at all** and just hold on tight, allowing the dog to pull without comment.

If you can adhere to this routine strictly, i.e. always enforcing your command once you have given it, and never giving the command if you can't be bothered to enforce it, your dog will learn quickly that you really mean it when you say "heel".

Step 5.
Be quite ruthless and insist on very exact heeling at this stage. If you allow your dog to creep forward even ever so slightly, you will be back to full scale pulling sooner or later.

The dog must also always sit when you halt, and you should let him know that you are deeply displeased if he does not.

Tell him off in a disgusted rather than an aggressive manner, using

phrases such as, "I don't believe it!! What on earth do you think you're doing?! I have never seen such disgraceful behaviour!".

Two or three weeks of effort will be rewarded with a dog who walks nicely by your side for the rest of his life - a real bonus for dog and owner alike.

And should he try his luck and start pulling again at a later stage, you will be prepared and know what to do about it.

Heeling with a Pram

Heeling with a pram is fairly easy - providing the dog walks to heel with you on command in the first place.

Teaching a dog to walk to heel and pushing a pram at the same time is virtually impossible. The dog ought to be taught seperately and should have a chance to practise with you on his own before having to walk behind a pram.

The correct position for your dog when you are pushing a pram is still by your side, not next to the pram or pushchair. In this position you will not take up the whole pavement and more importantly, you will not run over your dog's feet when you have to change direction suddenly.

A safety note; Never tie your dog's lead to your pram or push chair, either when walking or when parked outside a shop. This could be very dangerous if your dog is suddenly frightened or startled, or should decide to take off after a cat or another dog.

STEP 1

"Go to Bed!"

Sending a dog to his bed is a good way of preventing stress, trouble and strife as it is much easier for both dog and owner when the dog is removed from the scene than to have to command and reprimand him constantly.

It is taught in five easy steps; how long your dog will take to learn this depends on his willingness to co-operate and on how much time you can invest in his training.

Step 1.
Place some food in your dog's bed while he is watching. Take him back a few paces, holding his collar. Point to the bed, give a command (such as "Basket!", "Go to bed!" etc.) and let him go to eat the treat. Practise a number of times until your dog has become used to this "game" and understands the basic idea.

Step 2.
Still with a treat in the bed, send your dog to it from every room in the house. Practise until your dog does it happily and reliably every time.

Step 3.
Stand by the bed holding the treat in your hand. Send your dog to the bed as before, but this time make him lie down in it.

As soon as he is down, place the treat between his paws and praise at the same time.

Practise until the dog automatically lies down when you give the "Go to bed" command, rewarding and praising frequently.

Step 5.
Gradually start moving away from the dog while he is lying down in his bed.

Begin by moving only a step or two away and gradually extend the distance over a period of a week or two, until you can leave the room while the dog stays in his bed.

Practise this whenever possible. Sometimes reward the dog with a treat, sometimes with praise, but always go up to him to reward him when he is in his bed, because this is what we want to encourage.

Should he get up before you have decided to end the exercise, simply put him back in the bed, leave him for a very short time, then let him come out if he wants to.

The important part of this exercise is not the length of time the dog spends in his bed, but whether **you** are in control of the situation. It takes a few months for a dog to learn to stay reliably for long stretches in his bed, so do not expect too much to begin with.

Crate Training

A crate, or portable dog cage, has a hundred and one uses. It can provide a safe retreat for your dog in many situations, keep him out of harm's way, help with training problems, be used to transport him safely and provide a home from home for your dog when you're staying somewhere overnight.

A dog does not see a crate as a cage: "Oh dear I can't get out!", but as a cave or den: "What a relief, no-one can get in!" providing he has been accustomed to staying in it gradually, and also providing the crate is used sensibly.

There are a few rescued dogs who have had bad experiences in the past with crates or cages and will never be happy to stay in one, but these are an exception; most dogs really enjoy the comfort and safety a crate can provide.

Step 1.
Leave the door open at all times. At feeding time, place the bowl into the crate. Hold your dog's collar, give a command such as "In you go", "Crate" etc., and allow your dog to enter the crate to eat his food.

Step 2.
After about a week of the above, proceed as before but shut the door when the dog is inside the crate. As soon as the dog has finished his food, open the door to let him out.

A plastic...

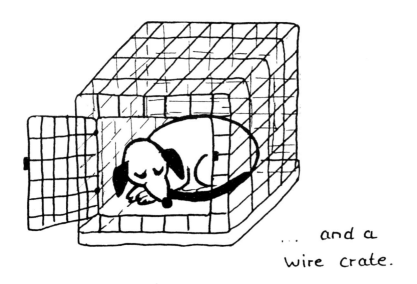

... and a
wire crate.

Step 3.
Place a chew, toy or bone in the crate. Using your usual command, let the dog enter the crate. Shut the door. Stay in sight and open the door after a few minutes - before the dog has become in any way unhappy or uncomfortable.

Step 4.
Over a period of one or two weeks gradually lengthen the time the dog stays in the crate with the door shut. Should he enter it without having being told to do so during the day, always let him know you are pleased and praise him sincerely.

Step 5.
Your dog is now crate trained. The crate should be available for your dog at all times and you can shut him in when and if this should be required.

Greeting Behaviour

Why do dogs jump up at people? We all know the answer - dogs jump in order to get closer to people's faces. This is how a puppy would greet a returning adult dog, jumping up and licking his muzzle, both as a greeting and as a food begging behaviour.

One of the nicest things about owning dogs is the sincere happiness they show when they greet us. This makes it doubly difficult for many owners as they feel it is wrong to punish the dog only because it is so happy to see them that it can't contain itself.

The reason why over excitable greeting behaviour is one of the most common complaints owners have about their dogs, lies in a basic misunderstanding.

Pushing an excited dog away and telling it off will lead to more displays of submission - i. e. more jumping up - rather than less.

Furthermore, as soon as you start to yell, push or shove, the dog will become stressed. In dogs this mostly manifests itself in even more excitable behaviour, such as jumping up and down, barking, leaping, wriggling or even wetting.

General Points.

Try to remove some of the stress involved by creating as calm an atmosphere as possible.

Ignoring the dog completely is the best long term method of reducing over excitable greeting behaviour.

At first this will not seem to work as the dog will redouble his efforts to gain your attention for a short time ("If at first you don't succeed, try harder" effect).

It is vital that you should pass through this phase without rewarding the dog for his efforts by giving in to him and paying him attention. The key to success is to pretend that the dog does not exist, no matter how hard he might be trying to convince you otherwise.

Over excitable greeting behaviour tends to occur with visitors, with family or with both.

Although the basic approaches to re-training your dog are the same, there are a number of differences in the practical application as you cannot explain the "ins and outs" of your dog training to every relative, salesman or acquaintance who might enter your house.

I. Greeting Visitors

With visitors the best method to achieve some measure of control over the dog whilst ignoring it at the same time is to put the dog on a longish lead before opening the door.

Hold the lead in one hand and stand on the rest, just near enough to the clip attached to the collar so the dog can stand up comfortably but cannot jump.

Pretend to ignore the dog from now on, even if you have to struggle to keep him in place.

Open the door to your visitor, ask him to enter, to ignore the dog and give him directions of where to go and to sit down.

Take your dog on the lead into the room once the visitor has sat down and begin a conversation, again pretending to ignore the dog even if you are struggling to keep him under control.

Do not command the dog or speak to him at all, just put your weight on the lead and stand tight. You will find that your dog will relax after a short period of time. Depending on your dog, you can then let go of the lead and allow your dog to go to the visitor. Should your dog show any objectionable behaviour, simply retrieve the lead and control the dog as before.

Within a week or so you will find that your dog has become accustomed to this new way of greeting visitors. You can then begin to wean him off the lead in stages, with the possibility of going back to more tighter control if your dog should have a relapse.

Weaning your dog off the lead works like this:

1. Hold the lead but don't stand on it.
2. Put the lead on but don't hold on to it.
3. Pretend to put the lead on.
4. Proceed without the lead.

The other alternative to training the dog, namely to lock it out in the garden or kitchen when visitors arrive, is not really a good solution.

Some dogs will learn to hate visitors because their arrival inevitably heralds a period of isolation, and in a dog's book there is no punishment worse than this, being a very companionable creature. Furthermore, the dog will not be able to guard you and your family if he is locked away when you answer the door.

So to train your dog, even if it seems a lot of trouble to begin with, is well worth doing, as a real effort for a couple of weeks will result in a well behaved dog for his lifetime.

II. Greeting Family

As with visitors, the key to teaching civilised greeting behaviour is to lower the "emotional temperature" of the greeting.

This process begins when you get ready to go out. Do not indulge in excessive farewells. No matter how short or long your absence is going to be, always say good bye to your dog in a friendly but off hand manner - "Going out now, Fido. Bye!" - and leave positively and happily.

On your return adopt the same slightly off hand manner. Open the door and quickly walk past your dog with a passing "Hi Fido, nice to see you."

Do not stop to pet or embrace your dog. Move out of your hall or passage immediately and into another room which is not usually the scene of frantic greetings (it all helps!). Take off your coat, put your keys away and unload any shopping, completely ignoring the dog and neither touching, talking to or commanding him in any way. Moving around quite briskly as you perform these tasks will help.

If there are any other persons present, make a point of saying hello to them before you address the dog. Once your dog has calmed down you can turn to greet him, but even then keep it quiet and easy.

This might sound a very contrived way of dealing with your beloved dog; don't worry, it is only necessary during a "training" period.

Once you have controlled your dog's over excitable behaviour you and your dog can go back to a normal spontaneous greeting.

Try to impress the need for this kind of routine on every person living in your home; remind them that this is necessary because of the baby. Some men are especially prone to spend ten minutes or so "after a hard day at the office" roughhousing with the dog in the drive or entrance hall and for your training to be successful it is vital that this should cease completely for time being.

Action Plan

1. Say your "goodbyes" briefly and cheerily to avoid leaving your dog in a state of emotional turmoil.

2. On your return, greet your dog in a very off handed manner, then pretend to ignore him completely, even if he has managed to ladder your tights or is hanging on to your left leg.

3. Greet any other members of your household before greeting the dog.

4. Get all other members of your household and regular visitors to co-operate.

5. Discourage any jumping up at other times by sharply commanding the dog to "sit" and not proceeding with whatever it was you were planning to do (putting on his lead, throwing a toy etc.) until he has obeyed.

Tricks & Games

Tricks and games are an excellent way to keep your dog's body exercised and his mind alive. They will also provide him with an opportunity to return to "centre stage" occasionally.

The more you teach your dog the quicker he will learn. It doesn't matter at all whether you are teaching obedience exercises or simple tricks; with each new skill he acquires you are adding a new dimension to your lives and making him a more rewarding pet to own.

A dog who knows a few tricks can also provide hours of entertainment for your child on a rainy day - and imagine how proud your child will be when your dog "performs" in front of some friends.

It's simple, easy and rewarding, so get started and turn your dog into your very own "Lassie"!

"Shake Hands!"
Easy to teach, this will soon become a firm favourite with everyone, as visitors immediately perceive a dog who gives his paw as harmless, cute and clever. It also procures attention for your dog which is after all what he loves the best.

Simply start by sitting on the floor with your dog and lightly touching a paw until he moves it. Praise and give him a treat straight away. Repeat this many times; your dog will soon learn to lift his paw for the reward and all you have left to do is to add the

command "Shake Hands!" each time and to hold his paw before giving him the treat.

Jumping

Every fit and healthy dog loves physical activity. Jumping over simple obstacles, through hoops or over your arms or legs is great fun for everyone and nothing could be easier to teach.

Begin by placing a simple obstacle (such as a broom handle) on the floor and encourage your dog to walk across it, giving a command such as "Hup!" at the same time. A piece of food thrown across the obstacle can be a good incentive for a dog to try hard at this new game.

Gradually raise the height until your dog can no longer walk comfortably across. At first he will try to clamber over the obstacle, but after a few attempts he will learn that it is easier to "bunny hop" - this is the beginning of his show jumping career.

You can steadily increase the height and introduce different obstacles such as hula hoops. Try constructing a show jumping course in your sitting room using every day objects such as flower pots and mop handles.

"Snifferdog"

Dogs have excellent noses and thoroughly enjoy using them. You do not have to own a Blood Hound for these games as even the most refined pooch has a sense of smell a thousand times better than any human.

This is how to teach your dog to use his nose on command. Over a period of time get your dog used to finding a favourite article on command ("Where's your toy? Find it!"). Start by placing the toy within easy sight and only gradually make it more difficult for your dog to find. Once the toy is not within sight anymore, hidden behind another object or in long grass for example, your dog will automatically start using his nose to find it. Once he sniffs for the toy and finds it reliably, you can then progress to the next stage, grandly named "scent discrimination".

Place the toy amongst litter in the park and tell him to find it. As dogs do not have very good eye sight, he will have to have a quick sniff to decide whether the object in front of him is his toy or an old can - this is what scent discrimination means. The reason we are using litter at this stage is that all objects in your own house or garden will smell of you and this would confuse him to begin with.

Once he can pick out his own toy reliably from a selection of other articles you can progress to turning other objects into a "toy' by rubbing a little of your dog's spit on them. In this way you could mark an ace of spades in a pack of cards - totally invisible to your spectators but standing out as clear as dayglow paint to your dog.

Asking all your guests to put down their car keys and telling the dog to pick out yours is another variant of this game. Yet another "amazing" trick is to mark a coloured ball as before and have your dog pick it out amongst others, which will truly astound your visitors as everyone knows that dogs are colour blind.

There are countless other variations to this game - the only limit is your imagination.

Retrieving
Basic retrieving is one of the best and most enduring fun games for your dog, providing the thrill of the chase, physical exercise and excitement all at once.

Some dogs are natural retrievers. others need a little more encouragement to begin with.

If your dog is not interested in retrieving at all, you might be able to get him to play by sitting on the floor, bouncing a ball (large enough not to be swallowed by your dog!) against a wall and saying something like "Boy, this is **fun**! Shame **Fido** won't play!" to yourself whilst totally ignoring the dog. Your dog might decide to join in after a time and you can build this up with lots of praise and encouragement into a proper retrieve.

Dogs who will chase the article but do not pick it up can be motivated by jerking an old sock tied to a piece of string along the floor. Few dogs can resist trying to take a bite at this "rat" which again can be build up into a retrieve.

Dogs who will chase and pick up the article but won't return with it can easily be taught by keeping them on the lead and exchanging the article for a piece of food, then throwing it out again straight away. Most dogs learn soon that the quicker they return the toy, the quicker they can have another go.

Balloons
Some dogs really love balloons and can become very adept at keeping them in the air for a long time - a great game to play indoors on a rainy day without any risk to the furniture.

If your dog has never encountered a balloon before, introduce him to one that is only slightly inflated and still very rubbery. This way he won't be frightened by a loud bang when he pops a balloon for the first time.

Frisbees
A dog catching a frisbee in flight is an impressive sight;

furthermore, a dog who chases and retrieves frisbees will never be short of exercise! Many dogs learn to do this with amazing accuracy. Teach your dog basic catching skills by throwing food or soft toys at him before you go on to something as hard as a frisbee.

Learning Games

Teach your dog to "sit" as quick as lightning and to drop "down" like a brick by playing this simple little game whilst watching TV in your arm chair.

Hold either some food or a toy, depending which your dog prefers, and tell your dog to "sit". Wait patiently until he has sat, then immediately throw the food/toy at him. Your dog will learn that the quicker he obeys your command, the quicker he will get his reward. This also works for the "down" command.

When your dog is getting good at this game, whisper the commands - your dog's hearing is much better than ours and it will teach your dog to listen carefully to what you're saying.

If you always throw the food/toy just over his head he will learn to move further away from you which will give you control over your dog at a distance; this can also be turned into a game to see from how far away your dog can still catch something thrown by you.

Appendix II

Check List

Check List

Use the Check List to pin point the areas where you might need to take specific action.

Go through the Check List carefully. If you are unsure about an answer, stop and test your dog's response rather than guessing what he might do. If the answer to any question is "No", refer to the appropriate chapter and Action Plan for training advice.

Chapter 1, Handling.

Can you touch your dog all over without him becoming aggressive or excited? [] yes✓ [] no

Can you bath and brush your dog? [] yes✓ [] no

Can you clip his nails, hold his ears and tail without him becoming aggressive or excited? [] yes✓ [] no

Chapter 2, Exercise.

Does your dog walk to heel on a loose lead? [] yes✓ [] no

Do you play with your dog? [] yes✓ [] no

Does your dog go out with other people on occasion? [] yes [] no✓

Can you think of entertainments for your dog other than walks? [] yes✓ [] no

Chapter 3, Food.

Can you touch your dog while he's eating?   [] yes✓   [] no

Can you take his bowl and bone from him
without him showing any resentment?   [] yes✓   [] no

Does he take treats without snapping?   [] yes ✓   [] no

Chapter 4, Toys.

Can you take a toy from your dog without
him showing any resentment?   [] yes✓   [] no

Does your dog ignore things on the floor
that don't belong to him?   [] yes   [] no ✓

Can you control your dog when he is
playing excitedly?   [] yes✓   [] no

Chapter 5, Sleeping Places.

Can you approach your dog in his bed
without him showing any fear or
resentment?   [] yes   [] no

Does your dog go to his bed when you tell
him to?   [] yes   [] no

Can you move your dog off the furniture

without him showing any resentment or
fear?   [] yes   [] no

Can you move your dog easily when he is
sleeping on the floor?   [] yes   [] no

Chapter 6, Jealousy & Attention

Can you ignore your dog for some time
without him trying to gain your attention?   [] yes   [] no

Can you cuddle a cushion without your dog
trying to push in?   [] yes   [] no

Is your dog used to being left behind when
you go out?   [] yes   [] no

Do you sometimes praise your dog when he
is just being good and quiet?   [] yes   [] no

Chapter 7, Hygiene.

Is your dog innoculated and are his booster
injections up to date?   [] yes   [] no

Has your dog been wormed recently?   [] yes   [] no

Is your dog clean and free of fleas and
mites?   [] yes   [] no

Is your dog in good health and condition? [] yes   [] no

Can you get by without having to brush and comb your dog for a month? [√] yes [] no

Chapter 8, Safety.

Do you have a dog guard in your car? [√] yes [] no

Are you always fully confident and unafraid yourself when dealing with your dog? [√] yes [] no

Have you given thought how to separate your dog and baby when you are busy? [√] yes [] no

Does your dog greet without jumping up? [√] yes [] no

Can you run with your dog without him trying to jump at you or bite your ankles? [√] yes [] no

Appendix III

Further Information

Further Information

1. For help with behaviour problems write to:

> The Association of Pet Behaviour Consultants
> (APBC)
> 50 Pall Mall
> London

for referral to a member practise in your area.

2. Books & Videos

Please note that many dog training books still available in shops and libraries are based on old "army style" training methods which are not always applicable to modern day companion dog training. The following books and videos are up to date and highly recommended:

Books:
Dog Behaviour - Why Dogs Do What They Do
Dr Ian Dunbar

Your Dog - Its Development, Behaviour and Training
John Rogerson.

Think Dog
John Fisher

Recommended VHS Videos:

The Dominant Dog
John Rogerson

Basic Obedience Training
Silvia Hartmann-Kent & Rowna Wyatt

Sirius Puppy Training
Dr Ian Dunbar

About the Author

Silvia Hartmann-Kent was born in Germany and moved to Great Britain in 1979. She is a Member of the British Institute of Professional Dog Trainers, an Associate Member of the Association of Pet Behaviour Consultants and Senior Obedience Instructor with Berwick Obedience Association.

She currently lives in East Sussex with her husband Brian Kent, their two sons Alexander and Stephen, and their dogs Rio and Sunee, German Shepherds, and Rani and Sweep, Miniature Poodles.

Index

Index